# DAVID AND THE GIANT

## Bible Bedtime Story

### BLUME POTTER

# INTRODUCTION

In a world where courage and faith are needed more than ever, there is no better bedtime story for your children and grandchildren than the timeless tale of David and the Giant. This book is more than just a retelling of the Bible story—it's an inspiring journey through the eyes of young David, who shows us that with faith in God, even the smallest among us can overcome the greatest challenges.

David and the Giant is crafted with care to capture the imaginations of children aged 3 to 8, bringing them closer to the values of bravery, humility, and trust in God. Each chapter is written in a witty and engaging style, perfect for young listeners and readers. These stories will not only entertain but also teach your little ones important life lessons in a way that is both fun and memorable.

As you tuck your children or grandchildren into bed, this book offers the perfect opportunity to share a moment of faith and reflection, reminding them that they are never too small to make a big difference. With David and the Giant by their side, bedtime becomes a time of inspiration, comfort, and the beginning of dreams filled with possibilities.

This book is not just a story—it's a tool to nurture a strong, faith-filled foundation in the hearts of your little ones. Make David and the Giant a cherished part of your family's bedtime routine, and watch as the lessons of courage, faith, and humility take root in the lives of those you love most.

# CHAPTER 1:
# THE LITTLE SHEPHERD BOY

In a quiet, sun-kissed valley, there lived a young boy named David. He was the youngest of eight brothers, the smallest of the bunch, but what David lacked in size, he more than made up for in heart. His father, Jesse, was a humble shepherd, and like his father, David spent his days tending to the family's flock of sheep.

David had a special way with the sheep. While his brothers were off doing important tasks, David stayed in the fields, watching over the sheep with a keen eye and a brave heart. He carried a simple wooden staff, and his sling, which he used to protect the sheep from any danger, hung at his side. But it wasn't the staff or the sling that made David special—it was his unwavering faith in God.

Every morning, as the sun rose over the hills, David would sit on a large, smooth rock, overlooking the fields. He would take out his harp, a gift from his father, and begin to play. The melodies he strummed were gentle and sweet, and soon, the sheep would gather around him, as if they, too, were soothed by the music.

David's songs were not just for the sheep; they were songs of praise to God. With each note, David's heart soared, and he felt a deep connection to the Creator who watched over him and his family. As he played, he sang words of thanks and love, words that floated on the breeze and filled the valley with a peaceful calm.

One bright morning, as David was playing his harp, his father called out to him from the house. David quickly placed his harp down and ran to see what his father needed.

"David, my son," Jesse said with a warm smile, "I have an important task for you today."

David's eyes lit up. He loved helping his father and was always eager to take on new responsibilities.

"I need you to take this food to your brothers who are with King Saul's army," Jesse explained, handing David a basket filled with bread, cheese, and roasted grain. "They are camped in the Valley of Elah, preparing for battle.

Take this to them and bring back news of how they are doing."

David's heart skipped a beat. He had never been to the army camp before, and the thought of seeing his brothers and the soldiers filled him with excitement. But there was something else—a feeling deep inside that this journey would be more than just delivering food.

"I'll go right away, Father," David said, taking the basket and slinging it over his shoulder.

Jesse placed a hand on David's shoulder and looked into his eyes. "Remember, David, God is with you, always."

David nodded, his heart swelling with the love and encouragement from his father. He knew that God was with him, just as He was with him in the fields, watching over the sheep.

And so, with a spring in his step and a song in his heart, David set off towards the Valley of Elah. The journey was long, and the road was dusty, but David didn't mind. He walked with a purpose, feeling a sense of adventure and the comforting presence of God guiding his every step.

As he neared the army camp, David could see the tents of the soldiers spread out across the valley. The sight was grand and a little intimidating, but David pressed on. He knew his brothers were somewhere in that camp, and he couldn't wait to see them.

But as David approached, he noticed something strange. The soldiers seemed uneasy, and there was a tension in the air. David wondered what could be troubling the mighty soldiers of Israel.

Holding the basket tightly, David continued on, not knowing that this simple task would soon lead him to face a challenge greater than he had ever imagined—a challenge that would require all the courage and faith he had.

And so, the little shepherd boy took the first steps of a journey that would change his life, and the lives of all who would come to hear his story.

# CHAPTER 2:
# THE FEARSOME GIANT

As David neared the camp, the sounds of clashing swords and the murmur of the soldiers filled the air. The once peaceful valley now buzzed with tension. Soldiers hurried back and forth, their faces marked with worry. David looked around, searching for his brothers among the bustling crowd.

It wasn't long before David found his eldest brother, Eliab. Eliab was a tall, strong man, a seasoned soldier, and he greeted David with a mixture of surprise and concern.

"David! What are you doing here?" Eliab asked, his voice sharp with worry.

"I've brought food for you and our brothers, from Father," David replied, holding up the basket. "But, Eliab, what's happening here? Why does everyone look so afraid?"

Eliab took the basket but hesitated before answering. "David, this is not a place for you. There's a warrior—no, a giant—named Goliath. He's a Philistine, and he's been challenging our army for days. He's the biggest man anyone has ever seen, and he's been mocking us, daring someone to fight him."

David listened intently, his eyes widening as Eliab continued. "No one dares to face him. He's too big, too strong. King Saul has even offered a great reward to anyone who can defeat him, but..." Eliab's voice trailed off, and he shook his head.

"But what?" David asked, his curiosity piqued.

"No one is brave enough to take the challenge. Goliath is not just any warrior—he's a giant, a true fearsome giant. His armor alone is heavier than most men could carry, and his spear is like a weaver's beam," Eliab explained, his voice filled with both fear and frustration.

David's heart pounded in his chest. He could hardly believe what he was hearing. A giant? A warrior so terrifying that even the bravest soldiers were too afraid to fight him? David's mind raced, but instead of fear, he felt something else—a deep, unwavering sense of purpose.

"Where is this Goliath?" David asked, his voice steady.

Eliab looked at David with concern. "You shouldn't be asking such questions, little brother. You're just a shepherd, and this is a battle for soldiers."

But David was not deterred. "Where is he?" he repeated.

Eliab sighed and pointed towards the far side of the valley. "He's there, across the field. Every day, he comes out and shouts his challenge, and every day, we stand here, unable to do anything."

David turned to look where Eliab pointed, and there, on the opposite side of the battlefield, stood a figure unlike any David had ever seen. Even from a distance, Goliath was enormous, towering over everyone around him. His armor gleamed in the sun, and his voice, deep and booming, echoed across the valley as he taunted the Israelites.

"Why are you all so afraid?" David asked, more to himself than to Eliab. "We are the army of the living God! Who is this giant that he should defy the armies of the Lord?"

Eliab frowned. "David, you don't understand. Goliath is a seasoned warrior, and we are but men. None of us can stand against him."

But David was not convinced. "Is there no one who trusts in God enough to face this giant?" he asked, his voice filled with conviction.

Eliab shook his head. "It's not just about trust, David. It's about strength, and Goliath's strength is beyond anything we've ever seen."

David's mind was made up. He couldn't understand how the army of Israel, God's chosen people, could be so fearful. Goliath might be a giant, but David knew something that perhaps the others had forgotten: no one was greater than God.

"I'll fight him," David declared, his voice strong and sure.

Eliab stared at David, shocked by his words. "You? David, you're just a boy! You can't be serious."

But David was serious. "I may be a boy, but I know that God is with me. He has helped me protect our sheep from lions and bears—He will help me defeat this giant too."

Before Eliab could respond, word of David's bold declaration began to spread through the camp. Soldiers whispered to one another, and soon, the news reached King Saul himself. The king, curious about the brave boy who had volunteered to face Goliath, sent for David.

As David was led to the king's tent, he felt a mix of excitement and determination. He knew that this was the moment he had been preparing for all his life. It wasn't just about defeating Goliath; it was about showing everyone that with God, all things were possible.

When David stood before King Saul, he spoke with confidence. "Let no one lose heart because of this giant. I, your servant, will go and fight him."

King Saul looked at David, surprised by his courage, but also concerned. "You are only a boy, and Goliath has been a warrior since his youth. How can you hope to defeat him?"

David smiled, his eyes bright with faith. "The Lord who delivered me from the paw of the lion and the bear will deliver me from the hand of this Philistine."

King Saul saw the determination in David's eyes, and though he was still uncertain, he knew that this boy was different. There was a strength in David that came not from his size, but from his faith. And so, with a nod, King Saul gave David his blessing to face the fearsome giant.

As David left the tent, he felt a sense of calm wash over him. The battlefield awaited, and so did Goliath, but David knew that he would not face the giant alone. With God by his side, he had nothing to fear.

The stage was set for the showdown that would echo through the ages—a story of a young boy, a fearsome giant, and the unshakable power of faith.

# CHAPTER 3:
# DAVID'S BRAVE DECISION

The camp was abuzz with whispers and murmurs as the news spread—David, the young shepherd boy, had volunteered to fight Goliath. The soldiers couldn't believe it. How could this boy, who had spent his days tending sheep, hope to stand against the mightiest warrior the Philistines had ever known?

King Saul himself was astonished by David's courage. As David stood before the king, his youthful face full of determination, Saul couldn't help but feel a mixture of admiration and concern.

"David," Saul began, his voice gentle but firm, "I see your bravery, but you must understand, Goliath is not like the lions or bears you have faced. He is a giant, a warrior trained in battle from his youth. How can you, a young shepherd, hope to defeat him?"

David's eyes met Saul's, and in them, the king saw something unshakable—a deep and abiding faith. "Your Majesty," David replied, "I have faced dangers before, and each time, God has delivered me. When a lion or bear came to take a sheep from the flock, I went after it and struck it down. The same God who protected me then will protect me now. Goliath may be a giant, but he is no match for the power of the Lord."

Saul sighed, seeing the resolve in David's expression. He knew that no words could dissuade the boy. "Very well," Saul said, "but if you are to go, you must go prepared. Take my armor and wear it into battle."

The king called for his armor, and soon, the attendants brought out a gleaming bronze helmet, a heavy coat of mail, and a large sword. They began to dress David in the armor, but as soon as the helmet was placed on his head, and the armor fastened around him, David felt weighed down. The armor was far too big and cumbersome for his small frame. He could barely move, let alone fight.

David struggled to walk, taking a few awkward steps before stopping. "I cannot go in these," he said, shaking his head. "I am not used to them. I cannot fight like this."

With that, David began to remove the armor. The soldiers around him exchanged nervous glances, wondering how David could hope to face Goliath without the protection of armor. But David knew that his strength did not come from metal or might—it came from his faith in God.

Once free of the heavy armor, David felt lighter, more himself. He took a deep breath and turned to the king. "I will face Goliath as I am, with what I know."

David reached for his sling, the simple but trusted tool he had used many times before to protect his sheep. Then, with determined steps, he walked to the nearby river. There, he crouched down and carefully selected five smooth stones, each one fitting perfectly into the palm of his hand. These stones, small and unassuming, would be his weapons against the giant.

With his sling in one hand and the stones in a pouch at his side, David rose and began to walk towards the battlefield. The soldiers watched in silence, their hearts heavy with doubt, but David's heart was filled with confidence. He knew that God was with him, guiding his every step.

As David approached the battlefield, Goliath's taunting voice boomed across the valley. The giant sneered as he saw the young boy coming towards him, armed with nothing but a sling and a few stones.

"Am I a dog, that you come at me with sticks?" Goliath roared, his laughter echoing off the hills. "Come here, and I will give your flesh to the birds and the wild animals!"

But David was not afraid. He looked up at the towering giant, his voice steady and clear as he called out, "You come against me with sword and spear and javelin, but I come against you in the name of the Lord Almighty, the God of the armies of Israel, whom you have defied. Today, the Lord will deliver you into my hands, and everyone will know that it is not by sword or spear that the Lord saves; for the battle is the Lord's, and He will give all of you into our hands."

With those words, David placed a stone into his sling and began to swing it. The sound of the whirling sling grew louder, and in one swift motion, David let the stone fly. The small, smooth stone sailed through the air, guided by David's skill and God's hand, and struck Goliath squarely on the forehead.

The giant's laughter stopped abruptly as the stone sank deep into his forehead. Goliath staggered, his massive frame swaying for a moment before he fell, crashing to the ground with a thunderous thud.

The entire battlefield fell silent, the soldiers of Israel and the Philistines alike watching in disbelief. The mighty Goliath, the fearsome giant, was defeated by a single stone.

David stood still for a moment, his heart pounding, his eyes wide with amazement. He had done it. With God's help, he had defeated the giant.

A cheer rose up from the Israelite camp, the soldiers shouting with joy and rushing forward. The Philistines, now terrified, turned and fled. The battle was over before it had even begun.

David, the young shepherd boy, had triumphed, not with armor or a sword, but with faith and a simple sling. It was a victory that would be remembered for generations—a story of courage, faith, and the power of believing that with God, even the smallest among us can achieve great things.

# CHAPTER 4:
# THE BATTLE BEGINS

David stood at the edge of the battlefield, his heart steady and his gaze fixed on the towering figure of Goliath. The giant was clad in heavy armor, his massive spear gleaming in the sunlight. Around him, the Philistine soldiers cheered, confident that their champion would easily crush the young boy who dared to challenge him.

As David stepped forward, Goliath's booming laughter echoed across the valley. "Am I a dog, that you come at me with sticks?" he jeered, his voice dripping with disdain. The sight of the small shepherd boy, armed only with a slingshot, seemed like a joke to the giant.

But David was not deterred. He felt no fear, for he knew that he was not alone. God was with him, guiding his steps and giving him strength. Without hesitation, David reached into his pouch and pulled out a smooth stone. He placed it in his sling and began to swing it, the whirling sound growing louder with each rotation.

Goliath took a step forward, his massive frame casting a long shadow over the battlefield. The soldiers of Israel held their breath, their hearts pounding in their chests. Could this boy truly stand against the giant?

With a sudden burst of speed, David ran towards Goliath. The giant's laughter faltered as he saw the determination in David's eyes. But before Goliath could react, David released the stone from his sling.

The stone flew through the air with incredible speed, a blur against the sky. It struck Goliath with pinpoint accuracy, sinking deep into his forehead. The giant's eyes widened in shock, his massive body swaying for a moment before he crumpled to the ground with a thunderous crash.

For a heartbeat, the battlefield was silent. The Philistines stared in disbelief, unable to comprehend what had just happened. The mighty Goliath, the fearsome warrior who had terrorized them for days, lay defeated by a single stone.

Then, a roar erupted from the Israelite camp. The soldiers, stunned by what they had witnessed, broke into cheers and rushed forward. The Philistines, now filled with terror, turned and fled, their confidence shattered.

David stood over Goliath's fallen body, breathing heavily but filled with a sense of awe and gratitude. He had done it. With God's help, he had defeated the giant. The victory belonged not just to him, but to all of Israel.

As the soldiers lifted David onto their shoulders, cheering his name, he knew that this moment would be remembered forever. The young shepherd boy had become a hero, not because of his strength, but because of his faith. And in that faith, he had found the courage to face the impossible and triumph.

The battle was over, but the story of David and Goliath had only just begun, a story that would inspire generations to come.

# CHAPTER 5:
# A HEART AFTER GOD

The echoes of the battle faded, and the valley that had once been filled with the sounds of fear and uncertainty was now alive with celebration. The soldiers of Israel cheered and praised David, lifting him high on their shoulders as they marched back to camp. The victory over Goliath was not just a triumph over a giant but a symbol of hope and faith for the entire nation.

But as the soldiers chanted his name, David's heart remained humble. He knew that it was not his own strength that had brought down Goliath. It was God who had guided his hand, and it was God who deserved all the praise. As the soldiers gathered around him, eager to celebrate their new hero, David raised his voice above the crowd.

"Give thanks to the Lord, for He is good; His love endures forever," David declared. The cheers of the soldiers grew even louder as they joined in the praise, realizing that their victory was a testament to the power of God.

King Saul, who had watched the entire battle with astonishment, approached David. The king's eyes were filled with admiration, but also with a deep respect for the young shepherd who had accomplished what no other man had dared to do.

"You have done a great thing today, David," Saul said, placing a hand on the boy's shoulder. "Israel owes you a debt of gratitude."

But David, ever humble, shook his head. "It was not I, my king. It was the Lord who delivered us. I am but His servant."

Saul nodded, understanding the depth of David's faith. The king knew that David was no ordinary boy; he was destined for something greater. Yet, David did not seek glory or power. His heart was content in serving God and doing what was right.

As the celebrations continued, David quietly slipped away from the crowd. He returned to the fields where he had once watched over his father's sheep, the place where his journey had begun. But as he stood among the familiar hills, David knew that he was no longer the same boy. He had faced a giant and had seen the power of God's hand at work.

Though he returned to his humble duties, David's heart was forever changed. The people of Israel now looked to him not just as a shepherd, but as a leader, someone who could guide them with courage and faith. And David understood that with God, all things were possible.

As he tended his sheep, David continued to sing his songs of praise, but now, his voice carried the strength of experience and the wisdom of faith. He knew that life would bring more challenges, more giants to face, but he also knew that with God by his side, he could overcome anything.

And so, the young shepherd boy who had defeated a giant continued to walk the path that God had set before him, with a heart after God and a faith that would one day lead him to become Israel's greatest king.